HTML for Beginners: Building Your First Website

Index

Module 1: Introduction to HTML

Welcome to Module 1 of our course, where we dive into the fascinating world of HTML (Hypertext Markup Language). In this first lesson, we explore the fundamental concepts of HTML, understanding its importance in web development and performing a practical exercise to create a basic HTML structure.

Lesson 1: What is HTML?

HTML, or Hypertext Markup Language, is the standard language used for creating and designing web pages. Developed by Tim Berners-Lee in 1991, HTML provides the basic structure of a web page, allowing developers to define and organize content through the use of elements and tags.

Key concepts:

1. **Marking and Structure:**
   HTML uses a markup approach to structure the content of a web page. This markup is achieved by using tags that surround different parts of the content. Each tag has a specific purpose and contributes to the overall organization of the page.

2. **Elements and Tags:**
   In HTML, elements are the fundamental components that make up a page. Each element is surrounded by labels, which indicate the start and end of the element.

For example, the `<p>` tag is used to define a paragraph, and the paragraph text is contained between the opening `<p>` and closing '</p>` tags.

3. **Nesting:**
   HTML allows nesting of elements, which means you can place one element inside another. This nesting ability is essential for creating complex and hierarchical structures on a web page.

4. **Attributes:**
   HTML tags can have attributes that provide additional information about an element. Attributes are included within the opening tag and can affect the behavior or appearance of the element. For example, the `href` attribute is used in the `<a>` tag to specify the URL of a link.

Exercise: Write a Basic HTML Structure

Now, let's put what we've learned into practice by creating a basic HTML structure. In this exercise, we will build the skeleton of a simple web page. Remember that every HTML page begins with the `<!DOCTYPE html>` declaration followed by the `<html>` element, which acts as the main container for the page.

```html
<!DOCTYPE html>
<html lang="es">
<head>
    <meta charset="UTF-8">
```

```html
    <meta name="viewport"
content="width=device-width, initial-scale=1.0">
    <title>My First Website</title>
</head>
<body>
    <header>
        <h1>Welcome to My Website</h1>
    </header>
    <none>
        <ul>
            <li><a href="#section 1">Section 1</a></li>
            <li><a href="#section 2">Section 2</a></li>
            <li><a href="#section 3">Section 3</a></li>
        </ul>
    </none>

    <section id="section 1">
        <h2>Section 1: Introduction to HTML</h2>
        <p>HTML, or Hypertext Markup Language, is the
basis for building web pages. Allows...</p>
    </section>

    <section id="section 2">
        <h2>Section 2: Elements and Labels</h2>
        <p>In HTML, elements are the essential building
blocks that make up a page...</p>
    </section>

    <section id="section 3">
        <h2>Section 3: Next Steps</h2>
        <p>Now that we have created our basic HTML
structure, you can continue learning about...</p>
    </section>
```

```
  <footer>
    <p>&copy; 2023 My Website. All rights
reserved.</p>
  </footer>
</body>
</html>
```

Breakdown of the year:

1. **DOCTYPE Declaration and HTML Element:**
   ```html
   <!DOCTYPE html>
   <html lang="es">
   ```
   We start with the DOCTYPE declaration to specify the version of HTML we are using, followed by the `<html>` element that acts as the main container for the page. The `lang` attribute indicates the language of the page.

2. **Header (`<head>`):**
   ```html
   <head>
     <meta charset="UTF-8">
     <meta name="viewport"
content="width=device-width, initial-scale=1.0">
     <title>My First Website</title>
   </head>
   ```
   In the header section, we include essential metadata. The `<meta charset="UTF-8">` tag sets the character encoding as UTF-8, which is widely used. The `<meta name="viewport" content="width=device-width,

initial-scale=1.0">` tag ensures correct display on mobile devices.

3. **Body (`<body>`):**
```html
<body>
  <header>
    <h1>Welcome to My Website</h1>
  </header>
```

The body of the page starts with the `<body>` tag. Inside it, we create a header (`<header>`) with a main title (`<h1>`).

4. **Navigation (`<nav>`):**
```html
<none>
  <ul>
    <li><a href="#section 1">Section 1</a></li>
    <li><a href="#section 2">Section 2</a></li>
    <li><a href="#section 3">Section 3</a></li>
  </ul>
</none>
```

We include a navigation section (`<nav>`) that contains a list not ordered (`<ul>`) with links(`<a>`) to different sections of the page.

5. **Sections (`<section>`):**
```html
<section id="section 1">
  <h2>Section 1: Introduction to HTML</h2>
```

```
        <p>HTML, or Hypertext Markup Language, is the
basis of

the construction of web pages. Allow...</p>
    </section>

    <section id="section 2">
        <h2>Section 2: Elements and Labels</h2>
        <p>In HTML, elements are the essential building
blocks that make up a page...</p>
    </section>

    <section id="section 3">
        <h2>Section 3: Next Steps</h2>
        <p>Now that we have created our basic HTML
structure, you can continue learning about...</p>
    </section>
  ` ` `
```

We divide the content of the page into sections
(`<section>`), each with a heading (`<h2>`) and an
explanatory paragraph (`<p>`). The `id` property is
used to link navigation links to these sections.

6. **Footer (`<footer>`):**
```
  ` ` `html
    <footer>
        <p>&copy; 2023 My Website. All rights
reserved.</p>
    </footer>
  </body>
  </html>
  ` ` `
```

We conclude the page with a footer (`<footer>`) that shows the copyright year and the name of the page.

Conclusions:

In this lesson and exercise, we have covered the fundamental concepts of HTML and created a basic structure for a web page. From the DOCTYPE declaration to organizing content with tags like `<header>`, `<nav>`, `<section>`, and `<footer>`, you've begun to understand how HTML serves as the skeleton of a page. Web.

This is just the beginning of your journey in web development. As we progress through the modules, we explore more advanced concepts, design techniques, and best practices to help you build effective and attractive web pages. Keep going with enthusiasm and continue building your HTML knowledge!

Lesson 2: Basic Tools for Coding in HTML

In this exciting lesson, we'll dive into the basic tools needed to code in HTML. From text editors to web browsers, each tool plays a crucial role in the web development process. Additionally, we'll go through a hands-on exercise to set up a simple development environment, giving you the hands-on experience you need to start creating your own web pages.

Essential Tools:

1. **Text Editor:**
   A text editor is the primary tool for writing and editing HTML code. There are many options available, from simple editors to integrated development environments (IDE). Some popular ones include:
   - **Visual Studio Code:** A free and open source editor with a clean interface, syntax highlighting and extensions for a personalized experience.
   - **Sublime Text:** A light and fast editor with syntax highlighting and an intuitive interface.
   - **Atom:** Another open source editor developed by GitHub, with collaboration and customization features.

2. **Web Browser:**
   Web browsers are essential tools for viewing and testing your web pages. Different browsers may interpret the code slightly differently, so it's important to test in several to ensure compatibility. Some common browsers are:
   - **Google Chrome:** With integrated development tools (DevTools) that facilitate debugging and code analysis.
   - **Mozilla Firefox:** Offers a robust set of development tools and is known for its emphasis on privacy.
   - **Microsoft Edge:** Microsoft's browser, which also includes advanced development tools.

3. **Browser Development Tools:**
   Development tools built into browsers allow you to inspect elements, debug code, and analyze page performance. These tools are crucial for identifying and correcting problems in real time. You can access them by

pressing F12 or by right-clicking on the page and selecting "Inspect" (in most browsers).

4. **Version Control System:**
   Using a version control system, like Git, allows you to track changes to your code and collaborate with other developers efficiently. Platforms such as GitHub, GitLab or Bitbucket offer services to store and manage Git projects online.

Exercise: Setting up a Simple Development Environment

Now, let's get to work. We're going to set up a simple development environment so you can start coding in HTML.

1. **Install a Text Editor:**
   Choose a text editor that suits your preferences. For this exercise, we'll assume you're using Visual Studio Code. You can download it from [Visual Studio Code](https://code.visualstudio.com/).

2. **Configure Visual Studio Code:**
   After installing Visual Studio Code, open it and customize the interface according to your preferences. You can install extensions to add additional functionality. Some useful extensions for web development include "HTML Snippets" and "Live Server."

3. **Create a Project:**

Create a folder on your computer for your project. Inside this folder, create an HTML file called `index.html`. You can do this from the terminal or file explorer.

4. **Open in Visual Studio Code:**
   Open your project folder in Visual Studio Code. You can do this by selecting "File" > "Open Folder" and selecting your project folder.

5. **Write HTML Code:**
   Inside Visual Studio Code, open the `index.html` file and let's start writing basic HTML code. You can use the following example:

```html
<!DOCTYPE html>
<html lang="es">
<head>
    <meta charset="UTF-8">
    <meta name="viewport" content="width=device-width, initial-scale=1.0">
    <title>My First HTML Project</title>
</head>
<body>
    <header>
        <h1>Hello, World!</h1>
    </header>
    <section>
        <p>This is my first HTML project. Welcome!</p>
    </section>
    <footer>
        <p>&copy; 2023 My First HTML Project. All rights reserved.</p>
```

```
    </footer>
  </body>
</html>
` ` `
```

6. **Save and View in a Browser:**
   Save the file and open your web browser. Drag the
   `index.html` file into the browser or right-click the file
   and select "Open with" > [Your browser name]. You
   should see your first web page with the message "Hello,
   World!"

7. **Explore Browser Development Tools:**
   Open the developer tools in your browser (you can do
   this by pressing F12) and explore the different tabs, such
   as "Elements" to inspect and modify the DOM, "Console"
   to view messages and errors, and "Network" to analyze
   requests and responses of the server.

Conclusions:

In this lesson, we have explored the essential tools for
coding in HTML. From choosing a text editor to setting up
a simple development environment, every step is crucial
to making the web page creation process easier. As you
progress on your web development journey, you will find
yourself using these tools on a regular basis and discover
how they complement each other to improve your
efficiency and productivity.

Remember, constant practice is key to skill development.
As you dive deeper into HTML coding, you'll be ready to

explore more advanced concepts and build more complex web projects. Keep coding and enjoy the learning journey!

Lesson 3: Basic Structure of an HTML Page

In this lesson, we dive into the basic structure of an HTML page. Understanding the anatomy of a page is essential for any web developer, as it provides the necessary framework to organize and present content effectively. Additionally, we will carry out a practical exercise where you will create an HTML page with a header and paragraphs, consolidating your understanding of the essential elements of HTML.

Structure of an HTML Page:

HTML, or Hypertext Markup Language, uses a hierarchical structure to organize the content of a web page. The basic structure consists of key elements including the document, header, body, and footer.

1. **Documento HTML (`<!DOCTYPE html>`):**
   - The `<!DOCTYPE html>` declaration indicates the version of HTML we are using (HTML5 in this case). This line should be placed at the beginning of each HTML document to ensure correct interpretation of the code by the browser.

2. **Root Element (`<html>`):**
   - The `<html>` element is the main container of the page and encapsulates all other elements. It can have a `lang` attribute to specify the language of the page.

3. **Header (`<head>`):**
   - The page header, defined by the `<head>` tag, contains metadata and links to external resources such as style sheets (CSS) or scripts (JavaScript). Here, we specify the character encoding, initial scale, and page title.

4. **Body (`<body>`):**
   - The body of the page, encapsulated by the `<body>` tag, contains the visible content of the page, such as text, images and links.

5. **Headers (`<h1>`, `<h2>`, ..., `<h6>`):**
   - Headings are used to structure content into sections. They range from `<h1>` (the most important) to `<h6>` (the least important). Good use of headings improves the accessibility and readability of the content.

6. **Paragraphs (`<p>`):**
   - The `<p>` tag is used to define paragraphs of text. Each paragraph closes with the closing tag `</p>`. This helps divide and organize content logically.

7. **Links (`<a>`):**
   - Links, created with the `<a>` tag, allow navigation between web pages or opening external resources. They can be included in text or images.

Exercise: Create an HTML Page with Header and Paragraphs

Let's apply what we learned and create a basic HTML page. Follow the steps below to build your own HTML document.

1. **Create a New HTML File:**
   - Open your favorite text editor (such as Visual Studio Code) and create a new file called `page.html`.

2. **Write the Basic Structure:**
   - Inside your file, write the basic structure of an HTML document:

```html
<!DOCTYPE html>
<html lang="es">
<head>
    <meta charset="UTF-8">
    <meta name="viewport" content="width=device-width, initial-scale=1.0">
    <title>My First HTML Page</title>
</head>
<body>

</body>
</html>
```

3. **Add a Heading and Paragraphs:**

- Inside the body (`<body>`), add a header (`<h1>`) with the title of your page and some paragraphs (`<p>`) with descriptive content. You can use the following example:

```html
<!DOCTYPE html>
<html lang="es">
<head>
    <meta charset="UTF-8">
    <meta name="viewport" content="width=device-width, initial-scale=1.0">
    <title>My First HTML Page</title>
</head>
<body>
    <h1>Welcome to My First HTML Page</h1>
    <p>On this page, we will learn the basics of HTML and how to structure content effectively.</p>
    <p>HTML, or Hypertext Markup Language, is essential for web development and allows us to create interactive web pages.</p>
    <p>Let's explore this exciting world of web development together!</p>
</body>
</html>
```

4. **Save and View in the Browser:**
   - Save the file and open it in your favorite web browser. Can

Do this by dragging the `page.html` file into the browser or by right-clicking on the file and selecting "Open with" > [Your browser name].

5. **Look at the Resulting Page:**
   - You should see your first HTML page with a header and several paragraphs. Congratulations, you just created your own website!

Additional considerations:

- **Attribute `only':**
  Be sure to use the `lang` attribute in the `<html>` tag to specify the language of your page. This helps browsers and search engines understand the content.

- **Character Encoding (`<meta charset="UTF-8">`):**
  Declaring character encoding is essential to ensure that special characters are displayed correctly. Always use UTF-8, which supports a wide range of characters.

- **Descriptive Titles (`<title>`):**
  The page title, defined in the `<title>` tag in the header, is what will appear in the browser tab. Use descriptive and concise titles.

- **Browsers and Tests:**
  Test in different browsers to make sure your page looks and functions as expected. This is especially important to ensure compatibility between different platforms.

Conclusions:

In this lesson, we explored the basic structure of an HTML page and performed a hands-on exercise to create a page with a header and paragraphs. Understanding the fundamental layout of an HTML document provides you with the necessary foundation to develop effective, well-structured web content. As you progress in your web development journey, you'll be ready to explore more advanced elements and design techniques. Keep practicing and enjoying the creative process of building web pages!

Module 2: Fundamental HTML Elements

Welcome to Module 2, where we explore fundamental HTML elements that are essential for effectively structuring a web page. In this initial lesson, we will focus on "Headings and Paragraphs." Understanding how to use these elements not only improves the organization of content, but also contributes to a clearer and more understandable user experience. In addition, we will carry out a practical exercise where you will use headers to structure a web page, putting into practice what you have learned.

Lesson 1: Headings and Paragraphs

Headers and paragraphs are fundamental elements in HTML that allow you to organize and present information in a hierarchical and readable way. Headings are used to define sections and subsections, while paragraphs are used to present blocks of text. These elements are the basis on which the logical structure of a web page is built.

1. **Headers (`<h1>` to `<h6>`):**
   - Headings are used to structure content and provide visual hierarchy on a web page. They range from `<h1>` (the most important) to `<h6>` (the least important). Each heading indicates a section or subsection, and is used to highlight key information.

```html
<h1>Level 1 Header</h1>
<h2>Level 2 Header</h2>
<h3>Level 3 Header</h3>
<h4>Level 4 Header</h4>
<h5>Level 5 Header</h5>
<h6>Level 6 Header</h6>
```

- Each heading level indicates a decrease in importance. For example, `<h1>` could be used for the main page title, while `<h2>` and `<h3>` could be relevant subsections.

2. **Paragraphs (`<p>`):**
   - The `<p>` tag is used to define paragraphs of text. Each paragraph begins with `<p>` and ends with `</p>`. This allows you to separate and organize the text logically.

```html
<p>This is a paragraph of text.</p>
<p>Paragraphs allow content to be divided in a clear and structured way.</p>
```

- Using paragraphs is essential to prevent the text from looking overwhelming. In addition, it makes it easier to read and understand the content.

Exercise: Using Headers to Structure a Page

Now, let's put these concepts into practice. Imagine you are creating a website about productivity tips. Your goal is to use headings to structure the page and provide a clear visual guide to the topics that will be covered. Follow these steps to complete the exercise:

1. **Create a New HTML File:**
   - Open your text editor and create a new file called `productivity.html`.

2. **Write the Basic Structure:**
   - Inside the file, write the basic structure of an HTML document:

```html
<!DOCTYPE html>
<html lang="es">
<head>
    <meta charset="UTF-8">
    <meta name="viewport" content="width=device-width, initial-scale=1.0">
    <title>Productivity Tips</title>
</head>
<body>

</body>
</html>
```

3. **Add Headings and Paragraphs:**

- Within the body (`<body>`), use headings and paragraphs to structure the page. You can use the following example as a guide:

```html
<!DOCTYPE html>
<html lang="es">
<head>
    <meta charset="UTF-8">
    <meta name="viewport"
content="width=device-width, initial-scale=1.0">
    <title>Productivity Tips</title>
</head>
<body>
    <h1>Productivity Tips</h1>

    <h2>1. Set Clear Goals</h2>
    <p>Define clear and achievable goals to maintain
focus and motivation.</p>

    <h2>2. Prioritize Tasks</h2>
    <p>Identify and prioritize tasks according to their
importance and urgency.</p>

    <h2>3. Organize your Workspace</h2>
    <p>Maintain a clean and organized space to
improve concentration.</p>

    <h2>4. Time Management Techniques</h2>
    <p>Explore techniques like the Pomodoro
Technique to increase efficiency.</p>

    <h2>5. Productive Breaks</h2>
```

```
    <p>Integrate short breaks to maintain energy and
creativity.</p>

    <h2>6. Learn to Delegate</h2>
    <p>Don't be afraid to delegate tasks when
necessary.</p>
  </body>
  </html>
  ```
```

4. **Save and View in the Browser:**
   - Save the file and open it in your web browser. Notice
how the headings structure the page and how the
paragraphs provide detailed information under each
section.

5. **Refine and Customize:**
   - Experiment with different levels of headers and adjust
the content as needed. You can add more sections or
customize the styles with CSS to improve the appearance.

**Additional considerations:**

- **Use Semantics:**
  When choosing headers, make sure you use the correct
semantics. A `<h1>` should represent the main idea of
the page, followed by `<h2>` for important subsections,
and so on.

- **Consistency in Styles:**
  Maintain consistency in the presentation of headers. You
can apply additional styling using CSS to improve visual
cohesion.
```

- **Accessibility:**
  Make sure your structure is accessible. The headers

 and well-organized paragraphs make reading easy for all users, including those who use assistive technologies.

Conclusions:
In this lesson, we have explored the importance of headings and paragraphs in structuring a web page. Using headings effectively provides a visual hierarchy that makes content easier to navigate and understand. The practical exercise has allowed you to apply these concepts while creating a page on productivity tips.

As you progress in your learning, experiment with different HTML elements and discover how each one contributes to building effective and attractive web pages. In the next module, we'll explain more fundamental elements of HTML to further expand your web development skill set. Keep exploring and enjoying the creative process of building websites!

Lesson 2: Lists (Ordered and Unordered)

In this exciting lesson, we explore HTML lists, an essential tool for organizing information in a clear and structured way. HTML offers two main types of lists: ordered lists and unordered lists. These allow data to be presented effectively, whether in the form of steps, highlighted elements or any set of information that has a logical sequence or relationship. Additionally, we will carry out a practical exercise where you will create lists to organize information, consolidating your understanding of this fundamental element of HTML.

Ordered Lists (`<ol>`):

Let's start by exploring ordered lists. These are ideal when you need to present information in a specific order, such as steps in a tutorial, sorting items, or any sequential content. The main tag for ordered lists is `<ol>`, and each element in the list is defined with `<li>`.

```html
<ol>
    <li>Step 1: Prepare the ingredients</li>
    <li>Step 2: Mix the dry ingredients</li>
    <li>Step 3: Add the liquid ingredients</li>
    <li>Step 4: Bake at 180°C for 30 minutes</li>
</ol>
```

In this example, we have created an ordered list to represent the steps to make a recipe. Each step is indicated by `<li>` (list item).

Unordered Lists (`<ul>`):

Now, let's shift our focus to unordered lists. These are useful when sequence is not important, but you want to present elements prominently. The parent tag for unordered lists is `<ul>`, and like ordered lists, each element in the list is defined with `<li>`.

```html
<ul>
   <li>Manzanas</li>
   <li>Plátanos</li>
   <li>Oranges</li>
   <li>Fresas</li>
</ul>
```

In this example, we have created an unordered list to represent a list of fruits. The lack of numbers or sequence indicates that the presentation does not follow a specific order.

Nested Lists:

In addition to simple lists, HTML allows list nesting, meaning you can include one list inside another. This is useful when you need to represent hierarchical information or categories within a list.

```html
<ul>
   <li>Rubbing</li>
   <ul>
      <li>Manzanas</li>
      <li>Plátanos</li>
      <li>Oranges</li>
      <li>Fresas</li>
   </ul>
   <li>Verduras</li>
   <ul>
      <li>Carrots</li>
```

```
        <li>Spinach</li>
        <li>Tomatoes</li>
    </ul>
</ul>
```

In this example, we have added two unordered lists inside a main list. This creates a more complex structure that can represent, for example, a list of categories (fruits and vegetables) with specific items in each category.

Exercise: Create Lists to Organize Information

Now, it's time to put what you've learned into practice. Imagine you are creating a page about tips for a healthy lifestyle. Your task is to use lists to organize different types of information in a clear and easy-to-understand way.

1. **Create a New HTML File:**
   - Open your text editor and create a new file called `healthy lifestyle.html`.

2. **Write the Basic Structure:**
   - Inside the file, write the basic structure of an HTML document:

```html
<!DOCTYPE html>
<html lang="es">
<head>
    <meta charset="UTF-8">
```

```
    <meta name="viewport"
content="width=device-width, initial-scale=1.0">
    <title>Tips for a Healthy Lifestyle</title>
  </head>
  <body>

  </body>
  </html>
```

3. **Add Lists to Organize Information:**
   - Inside the body (`<body>`), uses lists to organize different types of information related to a healthy lifestyle. You can use the following example as a guide:

```html
<!DOCTYPE html>
<html lang="es">
<head>
    <meta charset="UTF-8">
    <meta name="viewport"
content="width=device-width, initial-scale=1.0">
    <title>Tips for a Healthy Lifestyle</title>
</head>
<body>
    <h1>Tips for a Healthy Lifestyle</h1>
    <h2>Balanced Nutrition</h2>
    <ul>
        <li>Include a variety of fruits and vegetables in your daily diet.</li>
        <li>Eat lean proteins, such as chicken, fish and legumes.</li>
```

```
        <li>Limit your intake of processed foods and
added sugars.</li>
        </ul>

        <h2>Regular Physical Activity</h2>
        <ol>
        <li>Get at least 30 minutes of moderate exercise
most days.</li>
        <li>Combine resistance and cardio exercises for
a complete focus.</li>
        <li>Find activities you enjoy to make exercise
more sustainable.</li>
        </ol>

        <h2>Rest and Stress Management</h2>
        <ul>
        <li>Try to sleep 7 to 9 hours each night for
optimal recovery.</li>
        <li>Practice stress management techniques,
such as meditation and deep breathing.</li>
        <li>Find time for relaxing activities that you
enjoy.</li>
        </ul>
    </body>
    </html>
    ```
```

4. **Save and View in the Browser:**
   - Save the file and open it in your web browser. Notice
how the lists organize the information in a clear and
structured way, making it easy to understand the tips for
a healthy lifestyle.
5. **Refine and Customize:**
```

- Experiment with different nesting styles and levels

of lists to see how they affect the visual presentation. You can add more items to the lists or customize the styles with CSS to your preferences.

Additional considerations:

- **Use CSS Styles:**
  Consider applying CSS styles to improve the visual presentation of your lists. You can change the color, spacing, and other aspects to fit the overall design of your page.

- **Add Images or Links:**
  If relevant, you can add images or links within list items to provide additional information or related resources.

- **Maintain Consistency:**
  Maintain consistency in the presentation of lists for a consistent user experience. Use similar styles for similar elements.

Conclusions:

In this lesson, we have explored the power of HTML lists, both ordered and unordered, to organize information effectively. Lists are versatile tools that make it easy to present data in logical sequences or by highlighting key elements. The practical exercise has allowed you to apply these concepts while organizing tips for a healthy lifestyle.

As you progress in your learning, experiment with different HTML elements and discover how each one contributes to building effective and attractive web pages. In the next lesson, we explore another fundamental element: links and anchors. Keep exploring and enjoying the creative process of building websites!

Lesson 3: Links and Anchors

In this exciting lesson, we dive into the fascinating world of links and anchors in HTML. Links are the essence of web navigation, allowing us to connect internal and external pages, while anchors offer us the ability to direct us to specific sections within a page. Understanding how to create and use links is essential to building a smooth and consistent user experience on the web. Additionally, we will carry out a practical exercise where you will learn how to link internal and external pages, thus consolidating your knowledge in this crucial area of HTML.

External Links (`<a>`):

External links are essential to connect your web page with external resources, such as other web pages, files, images or even email addresses. The main tag for creating links is `<a>`, which means "anchor". Here is a basic example of how an external link is created:

```html
<a href="https://www.example.com">Visitexample.com</a>
```

In this example, `<a>` defines the start of the link, and the `href` attribute specifies the address to which the link points. The text between the `<a>` and `</a>` tags is what will be displayed on the page as the link text.

Internal Links (Same Site Pages):

To link internal pages within the same website, the process is similar. However, the address in the `href` attribute will be relative to the location of the current page. For example:

```html
<a href="page.html">Go to Page</a>
```

In this case, the link points to a page called `page.html` in the same folder as the current page.

Links to Local Files:

You can also link to local files, such as images, documents, or style files. The link structure remains the same:

```html
<a href="path/to/file/document.pdf">Download PDF Document</a>
```

Here, the link points to a PDF file in the specified folder.

Anchors (`<a>` with `id`):

Anchors are extremely useful when you want to target a specific section within a page. You can achieve this by using the `id` attribute in HTML to mark the target location and then link to that location. Let's look at an example:

```html
<!-- At the top of the page -->
<h2 id="home">Welcome to the Site</h2>

<!-- Somewhere on the page -->
<p>Interesting content...</p>

<!-- Link to anchor -->
<a href="#inicio">Go to Home</a>
```

In this example, the `<h2>` header has an `id` attribute of "start". The link at the bottom uses this `id` as a destination, allowing users to click the link to return to the top of the page.

Exercise: Link Internal and External Pages

Now, it is time to apply what you have learned in a practical exercise. Imagine you are building a website for an online library. Your task is to link the internal pages of your website and provide links to external resources, such as online books or library-related resources.

1. **Create New HTML Files:**

- Open your text editor and create new HTML files to represent different sections of your website. For example, you could have `home.html`, `catalog.html` and `resources.html`.

2. **Write the Basic Structure:**
   - Inside each file, write the basic structure of an HTML document:

```html
<!DOCTYPE html>
<html lang="es">
<head>
    <meta charset="UTF-8">
    <meta name="viewport" content="width=device-width, initial-scale=1.0">
    <title>Online Library</title>
</head>
<body>

</body>
</html>
```

3. **Add Content and Internal Links:**
   - Fill the content of each page with relevant information and create internal links to navigate between them.

```html
<!-- In the file home.html -->
<h1>Online Library</h1>
<p>Welcome to our online library. Explore our catalog and discover valuable resources.</p>
```

```
<a href="catalog.html">Go to Catalog</a>
<a href="recursos.html">Library Resources</a>

<!-- In the catalog.html file -->
<h2>Book Catalog</h2>
<ul>
   <li><a href="#libro1">Libro1</a></li>
   <li><a href="#book 2">Book 2</a></li>
   <!-- Other books... -->
</ul>

<!-- In the file resources.html -->
<h2>Library Resources</h2>
<p>Explore the additional resources we offer to enrich
your reading experience.</p>
<a href="https://www.librosexternos.com">External
Libros</a>
   ```
```

4. **Add Anchors and Internal Links:**
   - In the `catalog.html` file, add anchors for each book
and create internal links to allow users to jump to
information for a specific book.

```html
<!-- In the catalog.html file -->
<h2 id="libro 1">Libro 1</h2>
<p>Detailed information about Book 1...</p>
<a href="#inicio">Back to Home</a>
<h2 id="libro 2">Libro 2</h2>
<p>Detailed information about Book 2...</p>
<a href="#inicio">Back to Home</a>
   ```
```

5. **Save and View in Browser:**
   - Save the files and open them in your web browser. Browse through the internal pages and test the links to make sure they work correctly. Also check that the anchors take you to the correct sections of the page.

6. **Refine and Customize:**
   - Experiment with different styles and formats for links. You can add more content and links based on the needs of your online library.

Additional considerations:

- **Set Styles for Links:**
  Consider applying CSS styles to your links to improve visual appearance and provide visual feedback when they are clicked.

- **Use Relative Routes:**
  If your files are in different folders, be sure to use relative paths to link pages correctly.

- **Links to External Resources:**
  You can link to external resources, such as online books, articles, or library-related websites. Use the `target="` attribute _blank"` to open external links in a new tab.

Conclusions:

In this lesson, we have explored the importance of links and anchors in HTML to connect internal and external pages. Links are the backbone of web navigation, allowing us to explore content efficiently. The hands-on exercise has given you the opportunity to apply these concepts while building the structure of a website for an online library.

As you continue your learning, experiment with different HTML elements and discover how each one contributes to building effective and attractive web pages. In the next lesson, we explore another key element: incorporating images into your website. Keep exploring and enjoying the creative process of building websites!

Module 3: Images and Multimedia in HTML

Welcome to Module 3, where we explore the fascinating world of HTML images and multimedia! In this initial lesson, we will focus on how to incorporate images into a web page. Images are key visual elements that add engaging and meaningful content to your pages. Additionally, we will perform a practical exercise where you will learn how to add images to an HTML page, allowing you to immediately apply what you learn.

Lesson 1: Incorporate Images

Incorporating images into HTML is an effective way to improve the aesthetics and visual experience of a web page. The main tag for including images is `<img>`. This tag does not have a closing tag and uses several attributes to specify the image source, its description, and other visual details. Let's look at a basic example:

```html
<img src="path/to/the/image.jpg" alt="Image Description" width="300" height="200">
```

- The `src` (source) attribute specifies the path or URL of the image.

- The `alt` attribute provides descriptive text for the image, showing if the image does not load and is essential for accessibility.
- The `width` and `height` attributes define the dimensions of the image in pixels.

Exercise: Add Images to an HTML Page

Now, let's get to work. Imagine that you are creating a website for a travel blog, and you want to enrich your content by incorporating images of the destinations you have explored. Follow these steps to perform the exercise:

1. **Create a New HTML File:**
   - Open your text editor and create a new file called `travel blog.html`.

2. **Write the Basic Structure:**
   - Inside the file, write the basic structure of an HTML document:

```html
<!DOCTYPE html>
<html lang="es">
<head>
    <meta charset="UTF-8">
    <meta name="viewport" content="width=device-width, initial-scale=1.0">
    <title>Travel Blog</title>
</head>
<body>
```

```
    </body>
    </html>
    ` ` `
```

3. **Add Content and Internal Links:**
   - Inside the body (`<body>`), add relevant content for your travel blog. Use the `<img>` tag to incorporate images of the destinations.

```html
<!DOCTYPE html>
<html lang="es">
<head>
    <meta charset="UTF-8">
    <meta name="viewport"
content="width=device-width, initial-scale=1.0">
    <title>Travel Blog</title>
</head>
<body>
    <h1>My Travel Adventures</h1>

    <h2>Destination 1: Paris, France</h2>
    <img src="paris.jpg" alt="View of the Eiffel Tower
in Paris" width="800" height="600">
    <p>Exploring the charming streets of Paris...</p>

    <h2>Destination 2: Kyoto, Japan</h2>
    <img src="kioto.jpg" alt="Temple in Kyoto, Japan"
width="800" height="600">
    <p>Immersing myself in the culture and history of
Kyoto...</p>
```

```
    <!-- Add more destinations with images and
descriptions -->
    </body>
    </html>
    ` ` `
```

4. **Save and View in the Browser:**
   - Save the file and open it in your web browser. See
how images are incorporated into your website, improving
the visual experience.

5. **Refine and Customize:**
   - Experiment with different styles and formats for
images. You can add more content and links based on
your travel experiences.

Additional considerations:
- **Image Formats:**
   Be sure to use appropriate image formats, such as JPEG
for photos and PNG for images with transparency. This
helps optimize page loading.

- **Image Optimization:**
   Optimize your images for the web to reduce loading
time. Online tools can help you compress images without
significantly compromising quality.

- **Significant Alternative Text (`alt`):**
   Provide meaningful descriptions in the `alt` attribute to
improve accessibility. This is crucial for visually impaired
users and improves the page's SEO.

- **Dimensions Attributes:**

Specify the dimensions of your images with the `width` and `height` attributes to ensure a consistent layout as images load.

Conclusions:

In this lesson, we explored how to embed images into a web page using the `<img>` tag in HTML. Images are powerful visual elements that can significantly improve the presentation of your content. The practical exercise has allowed you to apply these concepts while creating a travel blog with images of fascinating destinations.

As you continue your learning, experiment with different HTML elements and discover how each one contributes to building effective and attractive web pages. In the next lessons of this module, we will explain more aspects of multimedia in HTML, including the incorporation of videos and audio. Keep exploring and enjoying the creative process of building websites!

Lesson 2: Links to Multimedia Resources

In this exciting lesson, we will delve into incorporating multimedia resources into HTML. Multimedia resources, such as videos and audio, are key elements to enrich the user experience on a web page. We will learn how to use the `<video>` and `< tag audio>` to integrate multimedia content, and we will carry out a practical exercise where you will insert a video or audio on an HTML page.

Multimedia Resources in HTML: `<video>` and `<audio>`

The `<video>` and `<audio>` tags in HTML allow the embedding of videos and audio files respectively. These tags are essential for creating interactive and engaging content for users.

Incorporation of Videos (`<video>`):

The `<video>` tag is used to insert videos into a web page. Here's a basic example:
```html
<video width="640" height="360" controls>
    <source src="video.mp4" type="video/mp4">
    Your browser does not support the video element.
</video>
```

- The `width` and `height` attribute specifies the dimensions of the video area.
- The `<source>` tag defines the location and file type of the video. You can provide multiple sources so that the browser chooses the best supported option.
- The `controls` attribute adds playback controls to the video, such as play, pause and volume.

Audio Incorporation (`<audio>`):

The `<audio>` tag is used to insert audio files into a web page. Here's a basic example:

```html
```

```
<audio controls>
    <source src="audio.mp3" type="audio/mp3">
    Your browser does not support the audio element.
</audio>
```

As with `<video>`, `<audio>` uses the `<source>` tag
to specify the location and file type of the audio, and
`controls` adds playback controls.

Exercise: Insert a Video or Audio into an HTML Page

Now, let's put what we've learned into practice. Imagine
that you are creating a website to promote a new music
album or a video tutorial. Follow these steps to perform
the exercise:

1. **Create a New HTML File:**
    - Open your text editor and create a new file called
`multimedia.html`.

2. **Write the Basic Structure:**
    - Inside the file, write the basic structure of an HTML
document:

```html
<!DOCTYPE html>
<html lang="es">
<head>
    <meta charset="UTF-8">
```

```
    <meta name="viewport"
content="width=device-width, initial-scale=1.0">
    <title>Recursos Multimedia</title>
  </head>
  <body>

  </body>
</html>
` ` `
```

3. **Add Content and Multimedia Resource:**
   - Inside the body (`<body>`), add relevant content for the promotion of your music album or tutorial video. Use the `<video>` or `<audio>` tags to embed the multimedia resource.

```html
<!DOCTYPE html>
<html lang="es">
<head>
    <meta charset="UTF-8">
    <meta name="viewport"
content="width=device-width, initial-scale=1.0">
    <title>Recursos Multimedia</title>
  </head>
  <body>
    <h1>Discover our New Album</h1>

    <p>We are excited to share our latest musical
production with you! Enjoy an exclusive preview
below:</p>

    <!-- Inserting a video -->
```

```
    <video width="800" height="450" controls>
        <source src="album_preview.mp4"
type="video/mp4">
        Your browser does not support the video
element.
    </video>

    <h2>Video Tutorial: Learn to Play a Song</h2>

    <p>Would you like to learn to play one of our
songs? Watch our tutorial below:</p>

    <!-- Inserting an audio -->
    <audio controls>
        <source src="tutorial_audio.mp3"
type="audio/mp3">
        Your browser does not support the audio
element.
    </audio>
  </body>
  </html>
  ` ` `
```

4. **Save and View in the Browser:**
   - Save the file and open it in your web browser. See how the multimedia resource is incorporated into your website, giving users an interactive experience.

5. **Refine and Customize:**
   - Experiment with different styles and formats for multimedia content. You can add more details about the album or tutorial to make the page more informative and attractive.

Additional considerations:

- **Multimedia Formats:**
  Make sure you use formats supported by most browsers. MP4 is widely accepted for videos, while MP3 is common for audio.

- **File Size Optimization:**
  Optimize the size of your media files to ensure fast page loading. Use compression tools to reduce size without compromising quality.

- **Additional Controls and Attributes:**
  Experiment with other available attributes to customize the appearance and behavior of media content. You can hide controls, set autoplay, and more.

- **Accessibility:**
  Provide meaningful descriptions for multimedia elements and consider including subtitles to improve accessibility.

Conclusions:

In this lesson, we explored how to embed multimedia resources, such as video and audio, into a web page using the `<video>` and `<audio>` tags in HTML. Multimedia resources are powerful tools to create interactive and attractive experiences for users. The hands-on exercise has given you the opportunity to apply these concepts while creating a music album promotion page and video tutorial.

As you continue your learning, experiment with different HTML elements and discover how each one contributes to building effective and attractive web pages. In the next few lessons, we will explain more aspects of web development, including interactive forms and advanced styling with CSS. Keep exploring and enjoying the creative process of building websites!

Lesson 3: Media Optimization for the Web

In this lesson, we dive into the fascinating world of media optimization for the web. Optimization is an essential practice to ensure that images, videos, and other multimedia elements on your website load efficiently, providing users with a fast and enjoyable experience. Additionally, we will carry out a practical exercise where you will learn how to compress and optimize images, ensuring that your multimedia content is ready to be consumed on the web.

Importance of Media Optimization:

Media optimization is crucial in web development as it directly affects the loading speed of a page. A fast website not only improves user experience, but is also a key factor in search engine rankings. Here are some reasons why media optimization is essential:

1. **User Experience:** Users prefer websites that load quickly. Optimization ensures that images and other multimedia elements do not slow down the page load.

2. **SEO (Search Engine Optimization):** Search engines, like Google, consider loading speed as a factor in ranking search results.Sites Faster websites tend to perform better in search results.

3. **Bandwidth Savings:** Optimization reduces the size of media files, resulting in lower bandwidth usage for both servers and end users.

4. **Accessibility:** Optimized web pages load faster, which benefits users with slower Internet connections or devices with limited resources.

5. **User Retention:** Visitors are more likely to stay on a website that loads quickly. Slow loading can increase bounce rate, meaning users leave the site before interacting.

Exercise: Compress and Optimize Images

In this hands-on exercise, you'll learn how to use simple online tools and techniques to compress and optimize images before embedding them on your website. Follow these steps to perform the exercise:

1. **Select Images to Optimize:**
   - Choose some images that you want to incorporate into your website. They can be product images, background photos, or any other type of graphic.

2. **Use Online Tools:**

- There are several free online tools that allow you to compress images without losing significant quality. Some popular options include TinyPNG, JPEG-Optimizer, and ImageOptim. Upload your images to one of these tools and download the compressed versions.

3. **Check Visual Quality:**
   - Before incorporating compressed images into your website, visually verify that the quality has not decreased drastically. Adjust compression settings as needed to balance file quality and size.

4. **Write the HTML Structure:**
   - Open your text editor and create a new HTML file for your web page. Write the basic structure of the document:

```html
<!DOCTYPE html>
<html lang="es">
<head>
    <meta charset="UTF-8">
    <meta name="viewport" content="width=device-width, initial-scale=1.0">
    <title>My Optimized Website</title>
</head>
<body>

</body>
</html>
```

5. **Incorporate Optimized Images:**

- Inside the body (`<body>`), use the `<img>` tag to incorporate the optimized images. Make sure you use the compressed versions you downloaded.

```html
<!DOCTYPE html>
<html lang="es">
<head>
    <meta charset="UTF-8">
    <meta name="viewport" content="width=device-width, initial-scale=1.0">
    <title>My Optimized Website</title>
</head>
<body>
    <h1>Explore Optimized Images</h1>
    <img src="optimized_image_1.jpg" alt="Image Description 1" width="800" height="600">
    <img src="optimized_image_2.jpg" alt="Image Description 2" width="800" height="600">
    <!-- Add more optimized images as needed -->
</body>
</html>
```

6. **Save and View in Browser:**
   - Save the file and open it in your web browser. See how optimized images load quickly, improving the speed of your website.

7. **Check File Sizes:**
   - Compare file sizes of original images with optimized versions. Note the significant reduction in file size, which contributes to faster loading.

Additional considerations:

- **Image Formats:** Consider the most appropriate image format for each case. JPEG is ideal for photographs, while PNG is preferable for graphics and elements with transparency.

- **Image Resolution:** Adjusts the resolution of the images according to the context of use. High resolution images may not be necessary in all cases.

- **Use of CSS:** Use CSS to apply styles and dimensions to your images. This provides more control over the design and makes it easier to adjust in the future.

- **Performance Testing:** Use online tools like Google's PageSpeed Insights to evaluate the performance of your website and get additional optimization suggestions.

Conclusions:

In this lesson, we have explored the importance of media optimization for the web and its impact on page loading speed. Image optimization is an essential practice to ensure a fast and efficient user experience. The practical exercise has allowed you to apply these concepts while using tablets and optimist images for your website.

As you continue your learning, keep in mind that media optimization is an ongoing practice. Always look for new tools and techniques to ensure your media loads efficiently. In the next few lessons, we will explain more aspects of web development, including advanced CSS techniques and creating

 of interactive forms. Keep exploring and enjoying the creative process of building efficient and attractive websites!

Module 4: Forms and Data Entry

Welcome to Module 4, where we dive into the exciting world of HTML forms and data entry! Forms are essential elements for interacting with users, allowing you to submit information and actively participate on your website. In this first lesson, we will learn how to create forms in HTML, and we will perform an exciting practical exercise: building a simple contact form.

Lesson 1: Creating Forms

HTML forms are elements that allow users to enter data and send it to a server for processing. The key elements that make up a form are `<form>`, `<input>`, `<label>`, and other related elements. Here is a basic structure of an HTML form:

```html
<!DOCTYPE html>
<html lang="es">
<head>
   <meta charset="UTF-8">
   <meta name="viewport" content="width=device-width, initial-scale=1.0">
   <title>Mi Formulario</title>
</head>
<body>

   <form action="/process_form" method="post">
     <!-- Form elements are placed here -->
```

```
    </form>

</body>
</html>
` ` `
```

- The `<form>` tag wraps all form content and has two key attributes: `action` (the URL to which the form data will be sent) and `method` (the HTTP method to be used, such as " get" or "post").

- Form elements, such as `<input>`, are placed inside the `<form>` tag. Each `<input>` can have a `type` attribute that defines the type of input (text, password, button, etc.).

- The `<label label>` is used to provide a descriptive label for a `<input>` element, improving accessibility and user experience.

Exercise: Build a Simple Contact Form

Now, let's put what we've learned into practice. Imagine that you are creating a website for your business and you want visitors to contact you. We'll build a simple contact form that collects the user's name, email, and a message. Follow these steps to perform the exercise:

1. **Create a New HTML File:**
   - Open your text editor and create a new file called `contact_form.html`.

2. **Write the Basic Structure:**
   - Inside the file, write the basic structure of an HTML document:

   ```html
   <!DOCTYPE html>
   <html lang="es">
   <head>
       <meta charset="UTF-8">
       <meta name="viewport"
   content="width=device-width, initial-scale=1.0">
       <title>Contact Form</title>
   </head>
   <body>

   </body>
   </html>
   ```

3. **Build the Contact Form:**
   - Inside the body (`<body>`), create the contact form using the tags `<form>`, `<label>`, and `<input>`. Defines fields for name, email, and message.
   ```html
   <!DOCTYPE html>
   <html lang="es">
   <head>
       <meta charset="UTF-8">
       <meta name="viewport"
   content="width=device-width, initial-scale=1.0">
       <title>Contact Form</title>
   </head>
   <body>
   ```

```
<h1>Contact</h1>

<form action="/send Message" method="post">
  <label for="name">Name:</label>
  <input type="text" id="nombre"
name="nombre" required>

  <label for="email">Email:</label>
  <input type="email" id="email" name="email"
required>

  <label for="message">Message:</label>
  <textarea id="message" name="message"
rows="4" required></textarea>

  <input type="submit" value="Send Message">
</form>
</body>
</html>
` ` `
```

4. **Save and View in the Browser:**
   - Save the file and open it in your web browser. Observe how the contact form is displayed. You can fill out the fields and click "Send Message", but currently, the form won't be sent anywhere as we haven't set up the action yet.

5. **Refine and Customize:**
   - Experiment with different attributes and styles to improve the appearance of the form according to the needs of your website. You can adjust colors, fonts, and margins to match the overall aesthetic.

Additional considerations:

- **`for` attribute on `<label>`:** The `for` attribute on the `<label>` tag is linked to the `id` attribute of the `<input>` element. This improves accessibility and allows users to click on the label to activate the corresponding field.

- **`required` attribute:** The `required` attribute on the `<input>` and `<textarea>` elements ensures that required fields must be completed before the form is submitted.

- **HTTP Method:** The `method` attribute in `<form>` specifies the HTTP method that will be used to send the data. "Post" is commonly used forms that send sensitive data.

- **Form Action (`action`):** The `action` attribute in `<form>` must point to the server URL that will process the form data. In this case, "/send Message" is a dummy URL that you must replace with the real action.

Conclusions:

In this first lesson of Module 4, we have explored creating HTML forms, an essential component of interacting with users online. The practical exercise has allowed you to build a simple contact form, collecting key information such as name, email and message.

As you continue your learning, consider exploring additional form elements, such as checkboxes, radio buttons, and drop-down menus. In the next lessons of this module, wewe will immerse in advanced forms techniques and we will explore how to process and validate form data on server side. Keep exploring and enjoying the creative process of building interactive websites!

Lesson 2: Types of Input Fields in HTML Forms

In this exciting lesson from Module 4, wewe will immerse in the various types of input fields that HTML offers to enrich the user experience in web forms. Input fields are essential for collecting specific information, and HTML provides a variety of types, such as text, password, number, and more. In this lesson,we will explore these types and we will carry out a practical exercise that will allow you to use different input fields in a form.

Common Types of Input Fields:

1. **Text Field (`<input type="text">`):**
   - This is the most basic type of input field and is used to collect text. It is ideal for names, addresses and any information that involves free text.

   ```html
   <label for="name">Name:</label>
   <input type="text" id="nombre" name="nombre" required>
   ```

2. **Password Field (`<input type="password">`):**
   - This type of field hides input characters and is used to securely collect passwords.

   ```html
   <label for="password">Password:</label>
   <input type="password" id="contrasena"
   name="contrasena" required>
   ```

3. **Electronic Mail Field (`<input type="email">`):**
   - Designed to collect email addresses and automatically makes some basic validations.
   ```html
   <label for="email">Email:</label>
   <input type="email" id="email" name="email"
   required>
   ```

4. **Number Field (`<input type="number">`):**
   - This field accepts only numbers and may include controls to increase or decrease the value.

   ```html
   <label for="age">Age:</label>
   <input type="number" id="edad" name="edad"
   min="18" max="99" required>
   ```

5. **Phone Field (`<input type="tel">`):**
   - Designed to collect phone numbers and may include specific features such as input masks.

```html
<label for="telephone">Telephone:</label>
<input type="tel" id="telefono" name="telefono"
pattern="[0-9]{10}" required>
```

6. **Close Field (`<input type="date">`):**
   - This type of field allows users to select a date from a calendar.

```html
<label for="date_birth">Date of Birth:</label>
<input type="date" id="date_birth" name="date_birth"
required>
```

7. **File Field (`<input type="file">`):**
   - Used to allow users to upload files, such as images or documents.
```html
<label for="file">Upload File:</label>
<input type="file" id="archivo" name="archivo"
accept=".jpg, .png, .pdf" required>
```

Practical Exercise: Different Types of Input Fields:

In this practical exercise, we will build a more complex form that uses several types of input fields. Imagine you are creating a registration form for an event. Participants must provide their name, email address, phone number and select date of birth. Additionally, they will be asked to upload a profile photo. Follow these steps to perform the exercise:

1. **Create a New HTML File:**
   - Open your text editor and create a new file called `registration form.html`.

2. **Write the Basic Structure:**
   - Inside the file, write the basic structure of an HTML document:

```html
<!DOCTYPE html>
<html lang="es">
<head>
    <meta charset="UTF-8">
    <meta name="viewport" content="width=device-width, initial-scale=1.0">
    <title>Registration Form</title>
</head>
<body>
</body>
</html>
```

3. **Build the Registration Form:**
   - Inside the body (`<body>`), create the registration form using different types of input fields. Define fields for name, email, phone number, date of birth, and profile photo upload.

```html
<!DOCTYPE html>
```

```html
<html lang="es">
<head>
    <meta charset="UTF-8">
    <meta name="viewport"
content="width=device-width, initial-scale=1.0">
    <title>Registration Form</title>
</head>
<body>
    <h1>Registration for the Event</h1>

    <form action="/registrar participante"
method="post">
        <label for="name">Name:</label>
        <input type="text" id="nombre"
name="nombre" required>

        <label for="email">Email:</label>
        <input type="email" id="email" name="email"
required>

        <label for="telephone">Telephone:</label>
        <input type="tel" id="telefono" name="telefono"
pattern="[0-9]{10}" required>

        <label for="date_birth">Date of Birth:</label>
        <input type="date" id="date_birth"
name="date_birth" required>

        <label for="profile photo">Profile
Photo:</label>
        <input type="file" id="foto_perfil"
name="foto_perfil" accept=".jpg, .png" required>
```

```
        <input type="submit" value="Registrarse">
    </form>
</body>
</html>
` ` `
```

4. **Save and View in the Browser:**
   - Save the file and open it in your web browser. Explore the registration form and see how the different types of input fields behave. You can simulate the registration process, but keep in mind that we haven't set up the form action yet.

5. **Refine and Customize:**
   - Experiment with different styles and attributes to improve the appearance and functionality of the form. You can add more fields depending on the needs of your event.

Additional considerations:

- **Phone Validation (`pattern`):** In the phone field, we have used the `pattern` attribute to specify a regex pattern that validates that only digits are entered and that the length is 10 characters.

- **`accept` attribute in File Field:** The `accept` attribute in the file field specifies the types of files that the user can select. In this case, we only allow files with `.jpg` and `.png` extensions.

- **Password Field Security:** When using password fields in registration forms, it is crucial to implement additional security measures, such as secure password storage on the server and password complexity policies.

- **Date of Birth and Accessibility:** Selecting the date of birth with the date field provides an easy to use interface. Make sure your form is accessible to all users, including people who use assistive technologies.

Conclusions:

In this lesson, we have explored the different types of input fields in HTML forms and applied this knowledge in a practical exercise to build a complete registration form. Each type of input field has its own characteristics and adapts to different data collection situations.

As you progress in your learning, consider how these input fields can improve the user experience and efficiency of data collection in your projects. In the following lessons of this module, wewe will immerse in advanced form validation techniques and server-side data processing. Keep exploring and enjoying the fascinating world of creating interactive forms on the web!

Lesson 3: Send Data Through HTML Forms

In this lesson from Module 4, wewe will immerse in the process of submitting data through HTML forms. Submitting data is a crucial part of user interaction on the web, and HTML provides the `<form>` element to facilitate this process. We'll learn how to set up a form to send data to an email address and do an exciting hands-on exercise to apply these concepts.

Configuration of the `<form>` Element:

The `<form>` element in HTML is the cornerstone for sending data from the client to the server. When setting up a form, there are several key attributes we need to consider.

1. **`action` attribute:**
   - This attribute specifies the URL of the server to which the form data will be sent. It can be an absolute or relative URL. In the context of this exercise, we will configure the form to send data to an email address.

2. **The ``method" attribute:**
   - The `method` attribute defines the HTTP method that will be used to send the data. Both Common methods are "get" and "post". For forms that contain sensitive data, such as passwords, it is recommended to use the "post" method.

3. **Input Elements (`<input>`, `<textarea>`, etc.):**
   - Inside the form, we use input elements like `<input>` and '<textarea>` for users to provide information. Each input element must have a `name` attribute that identifies the data when it is sent to the server.

Practical Exercise: Configure a Form

Send Data to an Email Address:

In this exercise, we will build a contact form that will allow users to send messages directly to an email address. Follow these steps to perform the exercise:

1. **Create a New HTML File:**
   - Open your text editor and create a new file called `contact_form_email.html`.

2. **Write the Basic Structure:**
   - Inside the file, write the basic structure of an HTML document:

```html
<!DOCTYPE html>
<html lang="es">
<head>
    <meta charset="UTF-8">
    <meta name="viewport" content="width=device-width, initial-scale=1.0">
    <title>Email Contact Form</title>
</head>
<body>

</body>
</html>
```

3. **Build the Contact Form:**

- Inside the body (`<body>`), create the contact form with the necessary elements for users to enter their name, email address and message.

```html
<!DOCTYPE html>
<html lang="es">
<head>
    <meta charset="UTF-8">
    <meta name="viewport" content="width=device-width, initial-scale=1.0">
    <title>Email Contact Form</title>
</head>
<body>
    <h1>Contact</h1>

    <form action="mailto:correo@dominio.com" method="post" enctype="text/plain">
        <label for="name">Name:</label>
        <input type="text" id="nombre" name="nombre" required>

        <label for="email">Email:</label>
        <input type="email" id="email" name="email" required>

        <label for="message">Message:</label>
        <textarea id="message" name="message" rows="4" required></textarea>

        <input type="submit" value="Send Message">
    </form>
</body>
```

```
</html>
` ` `
```

4. **Save and View in the Browser:**
   - Save the file and open it in your web browser. Explore
the contact form and see how it behaves when trying to
send a message. Note that the form action points directly
to an email address (`mailto:email@domain.com`).

5. **Interact with the Form:**
   - Complete the form fields and click "Send Message".
Depending on the email client settings on your device, an
email window may open with the data pre-filled.

Additional considerations:

- **`enctype` attribute:** The `enctype` attribute on
the form specifies how it will encode the data before
sending it to the server. In this case, we have used
`enctype="text/plain"`, which is a simple form of text
encoding for emails.

- **Limitations of `mailto`:** Using `mailto` in the form
action opens the user's default email client. However, this
technique has limitations and may not be supported by all
browsers and devices.

- **Server Actions:** In real-world situations, submitting
data through a form usually involves setting up a server
action. This can be a script in PHP, Node.js, Python or
another language that processes and manages the form
data.

- **Email Security:** When using the `mailto` approach, keep in mind that the data is sent through the user's email client and depends on that client's security settings.

Conclusions:

In this lesson, we explored how to set up an HTML form to send data via email. Although the `mailto` approach is simple, it is important to understand its limitations and consider more robust alternatives, especially in production environments.

As you continue to explore the world of web forms, consider learning about server-side form processing using technologies like PHP, Node.js, or Python. In the following lessons of this module, wewe will immerse in advanced server-side form processing and validation techniques. Keep exploring and enjoying the creative process of building interactive websites!

Module 5: Advanced Structure and Semantics in HTML

Welcome to Module 5, where we will explore advanced structuring and semantic techniques in HTML! In this inaugural lesson, we will focus on the use of `<div>` and `<span>`, two fundamental elements to organize and give structure to the content on a web page. We will carry out a practical exercise that will allow you to apply these elements effectively to improve the semantics and organization of your code.

Lesson 1: Using `<div>` and `<span>`

When it comes to structuring and organizing content in HTML, `<div>` and `<span>` are two essential elements that act as generic containers. Although they have no semantic meaning on their own, they are powerful tools when combined with CSS classes and styles to create flexible and accessible layouts.

1. **`<div>`: Block Container:**
   - `<div>` is a block element used to group other elements and create sections on your web page. It is extremely versatile and is the backbone of block structuring.

   ```html
   <div>
       <!-- Content grouped here -->
   ```

```
</div>
```

2. **`<span>`: Online Container:**
   - On the other hand, `<span>` is an inline element used to apply styles or scripts to a specific part of text without affecting the overall layout of a block.

```html
<p>This is a<span>specific text</span> inside of a paragraph.</p>
```

Both elements are essential for creating flexible layouts and semantic structures in HTML. By assigning classes to `<div>` and `<span>`, you can effectively customize and style specific sections of your page.

Practical Exercise: Apply `<div>` and `<span>`

Organize Content

Imagine that you are creating the structure of a home page for a blog. We will use `<div>` and `<span>` to organize and style content semantically. Follow these steps to perform the exercise:

1. **Create a New HTML File:**
   - Open your text editor and create a new file called `home_page.html`.

2. **Write the Basic Structure:**

- Inside the file, write the basic structure of an HTML document:

```html
<!DOCTYPE html>
<html lang="es">
<head>
    <meta charset="UTF-8">
    <meta name="viewport" content="width=device-width, initial-scale=1.0">
    <title>Blog Home Page</title>
</head>
<body>

</body>
</html>
```

3. **Organize Content with `<div>`:**
   - Create sections on your home page using `<div>`. Imagine you have a header, a featured article section, and a sidebar.

```html
<!DOCTYPE html>
<html lang="es">
<head>
    <meta charset="UTF-8">
    <meta name="viewport" content="width=device-width, initial-scale=1.0">
    <title>Blog Home Page</title>
</head>
<body>
```

```html
    <div id="header">
        <h1>Welcome to the Blog</h1>
    </div>

    <div id="highlights">
        <!-- Featured articles go here -->
    </div>

    <div id="sidebar">
        <!-- Sidebar content -->
    </div>
</body>
</html>
```

4. **Apply Styles with CSS:**
   - To visually highlight the sections, create a CSS file (you can name it `styles.css`) and link it in your HTML file. Applies styles to sections using classes.

```css
#header {
    background-color: #333;
    color: #fff;
    padding: 20px;
}

#featured {
    float: left;
    width: 70%;
    margin: 20px;
}
```

```css
#barra-lateral {
    float: right;
    width: 25%;
    margin: 20px;
}
```

5. **Organize Internal Content with `<div>` and `<span>`:**
   - Within each section, use `<div>` to group related content and `<span>` to highlight specific parts of the text.

```html
<div id="header">
    <h1>Welcome to the <span>Incredible</span> Blog</h1>
</div>

<div id="highlights">
    <div class="article">
        <h2>Article Title</h2>
        <p>Article Content...</p>
    </div>

    <div class="article">
        <h2>Other Title</h2>
        <p>Other interesting content...</p>
    </div>
</div>

<div id="sidebar">
    <div class="widget">
```

```
    <h3>Latest Articles</h3>
    <ul>
       <li><a href="#">Article 1</a></li>
       <li><a href="#">Article 2</a></li>
       <li><a href="#">Article 3</a></li>
    </ul>
  </div>
</div>
```

6. **Save and View in Browser:**
   - Guard both files and open them in your browser. Notice how the blog's homepage has taken shape with clearly defined and stylized sections.

Additional considerations:

- **Use of Classes:** In this exercise, we have mainly used IDs (`id`) to identify specific sections. However, in larger projects, it is common to use classes (`class`) to apply styles and structure content more flexibly.

- **Mobile Compatibility:** When designing your structure with `<div>` and applying styles, consider responsiveness to ensure an optimal experience on mobile devices and screens of different sizes.

- **Accessibility:** Make sure your content structure and organization are accessible to all users. Use appropriate semantic tags and provide clear descriptions when necessary.

Conclusions:

In this lesson, we explored how to use `<div>` and `<span>` to organize and structure content on a web page. These elements act as essential building blocks, allowing you to create complex and semantic designs. By combining them with CSS and attributes, you can achieve an attractive visual presentation and a logical structure in your HTML code.

As we progress through this module, wewe will immerse even further into advanced semantics and structuring techniques, exploring more specific elements that provide additional meaning to your content. Keep exploring and enjoying the exciting journey of building effective and visually appealing websites!

Lesson 2: Semantic Elements in HTML

Welcome to the exciting Lesson 2 of Module 5! In this lesson,we will explore HTML semantic elements, a powerful tool to give meaning and semantic structure to your web content. The semantic elements are notAlone They improve code understanding, but also play a crucial role in accessibility and SEO. In addition, we will carry out a practical exercise that will allow you to apply these elements on a web page.

Key Semantic Elements:

HTML5 introduced a series of semantic elements that provide clearer meaning to the document structure. Here are some key semantic elements that we will explore in this lesson:

1. **`<header>`: Page Header:**
   - `<header>` is used to represent the header of a section or the entire document. Contains introductory elements such as logos, titles and navigation.

```html
<header>
  <h1>Site Name</h1>
  <none>
    <ul>
      <li><a href="#">Start</a></li>
      <li><a href="#">About</a></li>
      <li><a href="#">Contact</a></li>
    </ul>
  </none>
</header>
```

2. **`<nav>`: Navigation:**
   - `<nav>` is used to represent the navigation section of the page. Includes links to other pages or sections of the site.

```html
<none>
  <ul>
    <li><a href="#">Start</a></li>
    <li><a href="#">About</a></li>
    <li><a href="#">Contact</a></li>
  </ul>
```

```
</none>
```

3. **`<article>`: Independent Content:**
   - `<article>` is used to represent independent, self-contained content, such as a blog article, news post, or comment.

   ```html
   <article>
     <h2>Article Title</h2>
     <p>Article Content...</p>
   </article>
   ```

4. **`<section>`: Generic Section:**
   - `<section>` is used to group thematically related content within a document. It can contain various elements, including headings, paragraphs, and other elements.

   ```html
   <section>
     <h2>Main Section</h2>
     <p>Section content...</p>
   </section>
   ```

5. **`<aside>`: Related Content:**
   - `<aside>` is used to represent content related to but independent of the main content, such as sidebars, notes, or ads.

```html
<aside>
    <h3>Barra Lateral</h3>
    <p>Related content...</p>
</aside>
```

6. **`<footer>`: Footer:**
   - `<footer>` is used to represent the footer of a section or the entire document. It contains information such as copyright, links to social networks or contact information.

```html
<footer>
    <p>&copy; 2023 Site Name. All rights reserved.</p>
</footer>
```

Practical Exercise: Using Semantic Elements on a Page:

Let's apply these semantic elements on a sample web page. Imagine you are creating the home page for a personal website. Follow these steps to perform the exercise:

1. **Create a New HTML File:**
   - Open your text editor and create a new file called `semantic_home_page.html`.

2. **Write the Basic Structure:**
   - Inside the file, write the basic structure of an HTML document:

```html
<!DOCTYPE html>
<html lang="es">
<head>
    <meta charset="UTF-8">
    <meta name="viewport" content="width=device-width, initial-scale=1.0">
    <title>Semantic Home Page</title>
</head>
<body>

</body>
</html>
```

3. **Use Semantic Elements:**
   - Use semantic elements to structure the home page. Add a header, a main section with articles, a sidebar, and a footer.

```html
<!DOCTYPE html>
<html lang="es">
<head>
    <meta charset="UTF-8">
    <meta name="viewport" content="width=device-width, initial-scale=1.0">
    <title>Semantic Home Page</title>
```

```html
  </head>
  <body>
    <header>
      <h1>User Name</h1>
      <none>
        <ul>
          <li><a href="#">Start</a></li>
          <li><a href="#">Blog</a></li>
          <li><a href="#">Contact</a></li>
        </ul>
      </none>
    </header>

    <section>
      <article>
        <h2>First Article</h2>
        <p>Contents of the first article...</p>
      </article>

      <article>
        <h2>Second Article</h2>
        <p>Contents of the second article...</p>
      </article>
    </section>

    <aside>
      <h3>Barra Lateral</h3>
      <p>Related content...</p>
    </aside>

    <footer>
      <p>&copy; 2023 User Name. All rights
reserved.</p>
```

```
    </footer>
  </body>
</html>
` ` `
```

4. **Save and View in the Browser:**
   - Save the file and open it in your browser. Notice how the home page is structured semantically, making the content easier to understand and improving accessibility.

Additional considerations:
- **`role` and `aria-*` attributes:** To further improve accessibility, you can use attributes like `role` and `aria-*` in semantic elements. These attributes provide additional information to assistive technologies.

- **SEO and Semantic Elements:** Search engines value semantics in HTML. The proper use of semantic elements can improve the visibility and ranking of your website in

 the search results.

- **Style with CSS:** Apply CSS styles to improve the visual presentation of your page. You can use classes and selectors to customize the appearance of each semantic element.

Conclusions:

In this lesson, we have explored the importance of semantic elements in HTML and how they provide meaning and structure to the content of a web page. By using elements like`<header>`, ``<no>`, `<article>`,

`<section>`, `<aside>`, and `<footer>`, you have created a well-structured and semantic home page.

Semantics not only benefits developers and designers, but also improves user experience and accessibility. As you continue your journey in web development, confidently integrate these semantic elements into your projects to create clearer, understandable, and more accessible websites. Keep exploring and enjoying the creative process of building effective and visually appealing websites!

Lesson 3: Meaning and Practical Application

Semantic Elements in HTML

In this exciting Lesson 3, we will delve into the meaning and practical application of semantic elements in HTML. Understanding semantics in web development is not only critical for search engines, but also improves code accessibility and understandability. We will carry out a practical exercise that will allow you to identify and apply appropriate semantic elements on a web page.

Importance of Semantics in HTML:

Semantics in HTML refers to the use of elements that have intrinsic meaning, making it easier for both developers and machines to understand the content. In addition to contributing to SEO and search engine ranking, the proper use of semantic elements improves accessibility by providing a logical and clear structure for users with assistive technologies.

Featured Semantic Elements:

1. **`<header>`:**
   - Used to represent the heading of a section or the entire document.

2. **`<none>`:**
   - Used to represent the navigation section of the page.

3. **`<article>`:**
   - Used to represent independent, self-contained content, such as blog articles.

4. **`<section>`:**
   - Used to group thematically related content within a document.

5. **`<aside>`:**
   - Used to represent content related to but independent of the main content.

6. **`<footer>`:**
   - Used to represent the footer of a section or the entire document.

Practical Exercise: Identify and Apply Semantic Elements:

Let's imagine you are creating an article page for a news website. The goal is to identify and apply appropriate semantic elements to improve the semantics and structure of the page. Follow these steps to perform the exercise:

1. **Create a New HTML File:**
   - Open your text editor and create a new file called `news_page.html`.

2. **Write the Basic Structure:**
   - Inside the file, write the basic structure of an HTML document:

   ```html
   <!DOCTYPE html>
   <html lang="es">
   <head>
       <meta charset="UTF-8">
       <meta name="viewport" content="width=device-width, initial-scale=1.0">
       <title>Semantic News</title>
   </head>
   <body>

   </body>
   </html>
   ```

3. **Identify Semantic Elements:**
   - Analyze the content of the news and identify the sections that can benefit from semantic elements.

   ```html
   <body>
   ```

```html
<!-- News Header -->
<div id="header">
    <h1>Incredible Scientific Discovery</h1>
    <p class="meta">Published on <time datetime="2023-04-15">April 15, 2023</time> by <span class="author"><span class="author"><span class="author"><span class="author"><span class="author"><span class="author"><span class="author"><span class="author">Name from the Author</span></p>
</div>

<!-- Main Content of the News -->
<div id="content">
    <p>Recently, a team of scientists made a surprising discovery that could change our understanding of the universe.</p>
    <!-- More content... -->

    <!-- Comments Section -->
    <div id="comments">
        <h2>Comments</h2>
        <div class="comment">
            <p><span class="user">User1:</span> </span> </span> </span> </span> </span> </span> </span> This discovery is amazing!</p>
        </div>
        <!-- More comments... -->
    </div>
</div>

<!-- Sidebar with Related News -->
<div id="sidebar">
```

```
        <h3>Related News</h3>
        <ul>
            <li><a href="#">New Advancement in Space
Research</a></li>
            <li><a href="#">Discovery in the Arctic: New
Unknown Species</a></li>
                <!-- More links... -->
            </ul>
        </div>

        <!-- Footer -->
        <footer>
            <p>&copy; 2023 Site Name. All rights
reserved.</p>
        </footer>
    </body>
    ` ` `
```

4. **Apply Semantic Elements:**
   - Use appropriate semantic elements to improve the
structure and meaning of the content.

```html
    <body>
        <!-- News Header -->
        <header>
            <h1>Incredible Scientific Discovery</h1>
            <p class="meta">Published on <time
datetime="2023-04-15">April 15, 2023</time> by
<span class="author"><span class="author"><span
class="author"><span class="author"><span
class="author"><span class="author"><span
```

```html
class="author"><span class="author">Name from the
Author</span></p>
        </header>

        <!-- Main Content of the News -->
        <article>
        <p>Recently, a team of scientists made a
surprising discovery that could change our understanding
of the universe.</p>
        <!-- More content... -->

        <!-- Comments Section -->
        <section id="comments">
            <h2>Comments</h2>
            <article class="comment">
                <p><span class="user">User1:</span>
</span> </span> </span> </span> </span> </span>
</span> This discovery is amazing!</p>
            </article>
            <!-- More comments... -->
        </section>
    </article>


        <!-- Sidebar with Related News -->
        <aside>
            <h3>Related News</h3>
            <ul>
            <li><a href="#">New Advancement in Space
Research</a></li>
            <li><a href="#">Discovery in the Arctic: New
Unknown Species</a></li>
```

```
            <!-- More links... -->
          </ul>
        </aside>

        <!-- Footer -->
        <footer>
          <p>&copy; 2023 Site Name. All rights
reserved.</p>
        </footer>
      </body>
      ` ` `
```

5. **Save and View in Browser:**
   - Save the file and open it in your browser. Notice how the news page has improved significantly in terms of semantics and structure.

Additional considerations:

- **Use of `datetime` and `class` Attributes:** We have used the `datetime` attribute to provide a machine-readable representation of date and time. Additionally, classes have been applied to style and select specific elements with CSS.

- **ARIA Roles and Attributes:** To improve accessibility, consider using `role` attributes and ARIA (Accessible Rich Internet Applications) attributes when necessary. These attributes provide additional information about the function and accessibility of the elements.

- **SEO and Semantic Elements:** By structuring your content with semantic elements, you are contributing to better ranking in search engines. Use elements like `<header>`, `<article>`, and `<footer>` to highlight key areas of your page.

Conclusions:

In this lesson, we have explored the meaning and practical application of semantic elements in HTML. Through a practical exercise, we identify and apply semantic elements such as `<header>`, `<article>`, `<section>`, `<aside>`, and `<footer>` on a news page, improving code understanding and user experience. Web development goes beyond simply creating pages; It involves creating meaningful and accessible experiences for users. By embracing semantics in your HTML code, you are taking significant steps toward building websites that are more understandable, search engine friendly, and accessible to all users. Continue exploring and enjoying the fascinating world of web development!

Module 6: Styles and Basic CSS

Welcome to Module 6, where we will explore the fascinating world of styles on the web! In this first lesson, wewe will immerse in the introduction to CSS (Cascading Style Sheets). CSS is the essential tool that allows us to give life to our web pages, applying styles and designs to make them visually attractive. We will carry out a practical exercise that will guide you in creating a basic style sheet to improve the appearance of a web page.

Lesson 1: Introduction to CSS

CSS is a styling language used to describe the presentation of an HTML document. While HTML focuses on structure and content, CSS takes care of visual appearance and layout. The separation of these two layers allows for more modular and efficient web development.

AsIt work in CSS?

CSS uses rules that apply to specific HTML elements. Each rule consists of a selector and a declaration block. The selector points to the HTML elements we want to style, and the declaration block contains the properties and values we want to apply.

```css
/* CSS Rule Example */
selector {
    property: value;
}
```

```
```

For example, if we want to change the text color of all paragraphs on a page to blue, the CSS rule would be as follows:

```css
/* Change Text Color to Blue */
p {
    color: blue;
}
```

Enlazando CSS a HTML:

There are three main ways to bind a CSS stylesheet to an HTML document:

1. **Online style:**
   - Styles are applied directly in the HTML tag using the `style` attribute.

   ```html
   <p style="color: blue;">This is a blue paragraph.</p>
   ```

2. **Internal style:**
   - Styles are included within the `<style>` tag in the `<head>` section of the HTML document.

   ```html
   <!DOCTYPE html>
   <html lang="es">
   ```

```html
<head>
    <meta charset="UTF-8">
    <meta name="viewport"
content="width=device-width, initial-scale=1.0">
    <title>Page with Internal Style</title>
    <style>
      p {
        color: blue;
      }
    </style>
</head>
<body>
    <p>This is a blue paragraph.</p>
</body>
</html>
```

3. **External style:**
   - Styles are stored in an external CSS file and linked to the HTML with the `<link>` tag.

```html
<!DOCTYPE html>
<html lang="es">
<head>
    <meta charset="UTF-8">
    <meta name="viewport"
content="width=device-width, initial-scale=1.0">
    <title>External Style Page</title>
    <link rel="stylesheet" href="estilos.css">
</head>
<body>
    <p>This is a blue paragraph.</p>
```

```
</body>
</html>
```
```

## Practical Exercise: Create a Basic Style Sheet:

We are going to apply what we learned in a practical exercise. Imagine that you are working on a blog home page and want to apply basic styles to improve its appearance. Follow these steps to perform the exercise:

1. **Create a New CSS File:**
   - Open your text editor and create a new file called `styles.css`. This file will contain our style rules.

2. **Write Style Rules:**
   - Inside the `styles.css` file, write basic style rules for the HTML elements you want to style. For example:

```css
/* Style the Header */
h1 {
    color: #333;
    text-align: center;
}

/* Style Paragraphs */
p {
    font-size: 16px;
    line-height: 1.5;
}
```
```

```css
/* Style Links */
a {
    color: #007BFF;
    text-decoration: none;
}

a:hover {
    text-decoration: underline;
}
```

3. **Link CSS File to HTML:**
   - Create a new HTML file (e.g. `index.html`) and link the external style sheet to the HTML using the `<link>` tag in the `<head>` section.

```html
<!DOCTYPE html>
<html lang="es">
<head>
    <meta charset="UTF-8">
    <meta name="viewport" content="width=device-width, initial-scale=1.0">
    <title>Blog with Basic Styles</title>
    <link rel="stylesheet" href="styles.css">
</head>
<body>
    <h1>Welcome to the Blog</h1>
    <p>Explore interesting articles and discover new ideas.</p>
```

```
    <p>Visit our <a href="#">home page</a> for
more content.</p>
    </body>
    </html>
    ` ` `
```

4. **Save and View in the Browser:**
   - Save both files (`index.html` and `estilos.css`) and
open them in your browser. See how the styles you've
defined are applied to HTML elements, improving the
appearance of the page.

Additional considerations:

- **Units of Measurement:** Properties like `font-size`
and `line-height` can be specified in different units, such
as pixels (`px`), ems (`em`), percentages (`%`),
among others.

- **Colors:** You can specify colors using names,
hexadecimal codes (`#RRGGBB`), RGB values (`rgb(255,
0, 0)`), or even predefined color names.

- **Pseudo-classes:** Pseudo-classes like `:hover` allow
styling to be applied when the user interacts with an
element, such as hovering over a link.

Conclusions:

In this first lesson of Module 6, we've explored getting
started with CSS and how to apply styles to HTML
elements. Through a hands-on exercise, you've created a
basic style sheet to improve the appearance of a blog

home page. This is just the beginning of your web design journey, and CSS will become your key tool in bringing your creations to life. Keep experimenting and exploring the endless possibilities of web styles!

Lesson 2: Apply Styles to HTML Elements

In this exciting lesson, wewe will dive deeper into the art of web design by learning how to apply styles to different HTML elements. The ability to style specific elements is essential for creating visually attractive and well-structured web pages. We will perform a practical exercise that will guide you through styling a variety of elements on a page,providing you with a Practical and valuable experience in the world of web design.

Selection of Elements with CSS:
Styling CSS is done by selecting specific HTML elements and defining associated style rules. CSS selectors are the tools that allow us to target specific elements and apply styles precisely. Some common selectors include:

- **Type Selector (`element`):** Selects all elements of a specific type (for example, `p` for paragraphs, `h1` for headings).

```css
/* Style for All Paragraphs */
p {
    color: #333;
}
```

- **Class Selector (`.class`):** Selects elements that have a specific class.

```css
/* Style for Elements with Class "featured" */
.outstanding {
    font-weight: bold;
}
```

- **ID selector (`#identifier`):** Selects an element with a specific ID.

```css
/* Style for the Element with ID "main-header" */
#main-header {
    font-size: 24px;
}
```

- **Offspring Selector (`element 1 element 2`):** Select elements `elemento2` who are descendants of `elemento1`.

```css
/* Style for Paragraphs within an Element with Class "container" */
.container p {
    margin-bottom: 10px;
}
```

- **Attribute Selector (`[attribute="value"]`):** Selects elements with a specific attribute and value.

```css
/* Style for Links with Attribute "target" equal to "_blank" */
a[target="_blank"] {
    color: #007BFF;
}
```

Practical Exercise: Styling Different Elements on a Page:

Let's imagine you're working on the home page of a travel website. Your goal is to apply styles to a variety of elements to create an attractive, cohesive look. Follow these steps to perform the practical exercise:

1. **Create a New CSS Style Sheet:**
   - Open your text editor and create a new file called `travel_styles.css`. This file will contain the style rules for our page.

2. **Define Style Rules:**
   - Inside the file `travel_styles.css`, defines style rules for various HTML elements on the travel site home page. For example:

```css
/* Style for Main Header */
```

```css
h1 {
    color: #333;
    text-align: center;
    margin-bottom: 20px;
}
/* Style for Description Paragraphs */
.description {
    font-size: 16px;
    line-height: 1.5;
    margin-bottom: 30px;
}

/* Style for Navigation Links */
.navigation {
    text-decoration: none;
    color: #007BFF;
    font-weight: bold;
    margin-right: 20px;
}

.navigation:hover {
    text-decoration: underline;
}

/* Style for Target Images */
.target-image {
    width: 100%;
    border-radius: 8px;
    margin-bottom: 20px;
}
```

3. **Link the Style Sheet to the HTML:**

- Create a new HTML file (e.g. `index_travel.html`) and link the external style sheet to the HTML using the `<link>` tag in the `<head>` section.

```html
<!DOCTYPE html>
<html lang="es">
<head>
    <meta charset="UTF-8">
    <meta name="viewport" content="width=device-width, initial-scale=1.0

">
    <title>Travel Site</title>
    <link rel="stylesheet" href="estilos_viajes.css">
</head>
<body>
    <h1>Welcome to Our Travel Site</h1>
    <p class="description">Discover fascinating places and create unforgettable memories with our incredible travel offers.</p>
    <a href="#" class="navigation">Explore Destinations</a>
    <a href="#" class="navigation">Special Offers</a>

    <h2>Featured Destination</h2>
    <img src="destination.jpg" alt="Featured destination" class="destination-image">
    <p class="description">Embark on a unique adventure in this impressive destination. Book now and live an unparalleled experience!</p>

    <!-- More content... -->
```

```
    </body>
    </html>
    ```
```

4. **Save and View in the Browser:**
   - Guard both files (`index_travel.html` and `travel_styles.css`) and open them in your browser. See how the styles you've defined transform the look and feel of your travel site's home page.

**Additional considerations:**

- **Box Model:** When applying styles, keep in mind the `box model` which describes how the total size of an element is calculated. This model includes the content, padding, border, and margin dimensions.
- **Colors and Fonts:** Experiment with different colors and font sizes to achieve the desired look. You can use hexadecimal values, color names, or even integrate custom fonts.

- **Responsive Design:** Consider implementing styles that adapt to different screen sizes to ensure an optimal user experience on mobile and desktop devices.

**Conclusions:**

In this lesson, we have explored applying styles to different HTML elements by defining style rules with CSS. Through a hands-on exercise, you learned how to select specific elements and apply custom styles to improve the appearance of a web page. The ability to style elements
```

precisely is essential for any web designer, and with practice and experimentation, you will be able to create visually striking and attractive web pages. Keep exploring and unleashing your creativity in the world of web design!

Lesson 3: Best Practices in Web Design

In this lesson,we will explore recommended practices in web design that will help you create more effective, accessible and attractive pages for users. In addition, we will carry out a practical exercise in which you will apply these practices to improve the design of a specific page. Let's move on and discover how to raise the quality of your web creations by implementing good practices.
1. Responsive Design:

The increasing diversity of devices used to access the web makes responsive design essential. This practice involves creating web pages that adapt fluidly to different screen sizes, from desktop to mobile devices. Using relative units, such as percentages and em units, and applying media queries are key steps to achieving a responsive design.

Practical Exercise - Responsive Design:

Imagine you have an existing website and your goal is to make it more mobile-friendly. Follow these steps for the exercise:

1. **Add Viewport Meta Tag:**

- In the `<head>` section of your HTML file, be sure to include the following viewport meta tag to control scaling on mobile devices:

```html
<meta name="viewport" content="width=device-width, initial-scale=1.0">
```

2. **Apply Media Queries:**
   - In your CSS style sheet,use media queries to adjust the layout on different screen sizes. For example:

```css
/* Styles for Large Screens */
@media screen and (min-width: 768px) {
    /* Add specific styles for larger screens */
}

/* Styles for Small Screens (Mobile Devices) */
@media screen and (max-width: 767px) {
    /* Add specific styles for smaller screens */
}
```

3. **Test on Mobile Devices:**
   - Save your files and test the page on mobile devices to make sure it looks correct and is easy to navigate.

2. Intuitive Navigation:

Good navigation is essential so that users can easily find the information they are looking for. Use clear and consistent navigation menus. Consider implementing single-page navigation to improve the user experience, especially on smaller websites.

Practical Exercise - Intuitive Navigation:

Let's say you work on a small business website and want to improve navigation. Follow these steps for the exercise:

1. **Create a Navigation Menu:**
   - Add a clear, easy-to-use navigation menu at the top of your page. Use semantic tags like `<nav>` and `<ul>` to structure the menu.

```html
<none>
  <ul>
     <li><a href="#inicio">Start</a></li>
     <li><a href="#services">Services</a></li>
     <li><a href="#we">We</a></li>
     <li><a href="#contact">Contact</a></li>
  </ul>
</none>
```

2. **Add Anchors on the Page:**
   - In your content, add anchor tags (`<a>`) with corresponding `href` attributes to allow smooth navigation between sections.

```html
<section id="home">
   <!-- Contents of the "Home" section -->
```

```
</section>

<section id="services">
  <!-- Contents of the "Services" section -->
</section>

<!-- More sections... -->
```

3. **Style the Navigation Menu:**
   - Use your CSS style sheet to style the navigation menu and make it attractive and easy to use.

```css
are not {
    background-color: #333;
    padding: 10px;
}

ul {
    list-style-type: none;
    margin: 0;
    padding: 0;
    display: flex;
    justify-content: space-around;
}

that {
    display: inline;
}

a {
    text-decoration: none;
```

```
      color: #fff;
    }
     ` ` `
```

4

. **Test Navigation:**
  - Save your files and try browsing. Make sure links work correctly and navigation is intuitive.

3. Web Accessibility:

Accessible web design is essential to ensuring that everyone, regardless of their abilities or disabilities, can access and use your site. Use semantic tags correctly, provide alternative descriptions for images (`alt`), and make sure your site is keyboard navigable.

Practical Exercise - Web Accessibility:

Imagine you are working on a nonprofit organization's website and want to improve accessibility. Follow these steps for the exercise:

1. **Semantic Tags:**
  - Review your HTML code and make sure you use appropriate semantic tags. For example, use `<header>`, `<nav>`, `<main>`, `<section>`, `<article>`, and `<footer>` meaningfully.
```
   ` ` `html
   <header>
     <!-- Header content -->
```

```
</header>

<none>
  <!-- Navigation menu -->
</none>

<main>
  <!-- Main content of the site -->
</main>

<footer>
  <!-- Footer content -->
</footer>
```

2. **Alternative Descriptions for Images:**
   - Add alternative descriptions to all images using the `alt` attribute. Provide concise and meaningful descriptions.

```html
<img src="image.jpg" alt="Woman enjoying nature in a forest">
```

3. **Keyboard Navigation:**
   - Make sure navigation and interaction on your site can be done using the keyboard. Try navigating and clicking on elements using only the arrow keys and the Enter key.

4. **Accessibility Tests:**

- Use online tools or browser extensions to perform accessibility testing on your site. Adjust your code as necessary to improve accessibility.

4. Legible Typography:
The choice of font is crucial for the readability of your content. Use legible fonts and make sure the text size is comfortable to read. Maintain a good contrast ratio between text and background to improve visibility.

Practical Exercise - Legible Typography:
Let's say you're working on a blog design and want to improve the readability of your text. Follow these steps for the exercise:

1. **Select Readable Fonts:**
   - In your CSS style sheet, choose fonts that are easy to read on different sizes and devices. For example:

```css
body {
    font-family: 'Helvetica', sans-serif;
    font-size: 16px;
    line-height: 1.6;
}
```

2. **Adjust Spacing and Line Spacing:**
   - Adjust line-height to improve readability. Make sure there is enough space between the lines.

```css
body {
```

```
    line-height: 1.6;
  }
  ` ` `
```

3. **Color Contrast:**
   - Maintain good contrast between text and background to improve visibility. Make sure the text is clearly legible.

```css
   ` ` `css
   body {
     color: #333;
     background-color: #fff;
   }
   ` ` `
```

4. **Test on Various Devices:**
   - Save your files and test text readability on different devices. Adjust the font size if necessary to ensure a comfortable reading experience.

5. Image Optimization:

Image optimization is crucial to ensuring fast loading times. Use appropriate image formats (such as JPEG for photographs and PNG for images with transparency), compress images to reduce file size, and use image sizes appropriate for use on the web.

Practical Exercise - Image Optimization:

Imagine you're working on an online portfolio and want to optimize images for fast loading. Follow these steps for the exercise:

1. **Select the Correct Image Format:**
   - Choose the right image format for your needs. Use JPEG for photographs and PNG for images with transparency.

```html
<img src="foto.jpg" alt="Photography of an urban landscape" />
<img src="icon.png" alt="Tool icon" />
```

2. **Compress Images:**
   - Use online tools or image editing software to compress your files before uploading them to the server.

3. **Define Image Sizes:**
   - Adjust the size of images according to the available space in your design. Avoid uploading images larger than necessary.

```css
img {
    max-width: 100%;
    height: auto;
}
```

4. **Loading Speed Tests:**
   - Use tools like PageSpeed Insights or Lighthouse to evaluate your page loading speed and make adjustments based on recommendations.

Conclusions:

In this lesson, we've explored various web design best practices ranging from responsiveness and intuitive navigation to accessibility, readable typography, and image optimization. These practices are essential to creating effective and engaging web experiences for users.

Through hands-on exercises, you've applied these best practices to a specific context, giving you tangible, hands-on experience implementing these concepts in the real world of web design. As you advance in your web development career, continue exploring new practices and techniques to constantly improve your skills and deliver exceptional web experiences. Keep designing and creating with passion!

Glossary

HTML for Beginners: Building Your First Website. This glossary provides key definitions of terms related to HTML and web development:

1. HTML (Hypertext Markup Language):
Markup language used to structure the content of a web page. It consists of tags that describe the function of different parts of the content.

2. HTML tag:
Fundamental element of HTML that defines and structures the content. Tags usually have an opening <tag> and a closing </tag>.

3. Element:
Combination of an opening tag, content and a closing tag. It can contain text, other elements, or be empty.

4. Attribute:
Additional information provided to a tag to modify its behavior or appearance. It is specified within the opening tag.

5. Website:
Document or resource on the web that may contain text, images, links and other elements. It is built using HTML.

6. HTML Document:
File that contains HTML code and is interpreted to render a web page in a browser.

7. Web Browser:
Application that allows users to access the web and view web pages. Common examples include Chrome, Firefox and Safari.

8. Marked:
The process of adding tags to content to structure and format it. In HTML, markup defines the appearance and function of different parts of a web page.

9. Header:
An element that provides structural information about a section, such as headings and subheadings. It is defined with <h1> to <h6> tags.

10. Paragraph:
- Elements used to structure and present text. It is defined with the <p> tag.

11. Link (Hyperlink):
- Element that allows users to navigate between web pages. It is defined with the <a> tag and the href attribute.

12. Ordered List (<ol>) and Unordered List (<ul>):
- Elements that create ordered and unordered lists, respectively. They use <li> tags for list items.

13. Image:
- Element used to display graphics or photographs on a web page. It is defined with the <img> tag and uses the src attribute to specify the image source.

14. Form:
- Element that collects user information. It is defined with the <form> tag and can contain elements such as text fields, buttons, and checkboxes.

15. CSS (Cascading Style Sheets):
- Language used to apply styles and layout to HTML documents. Allows you to control the presentation and appearance of a web page.

16. Responsiveness:
- Web design that adapts to different screen sizes, guaranteeing an optimal user experience on mobile and desktop devices.

17. Web Accessibility:
- Practice of designing and developing web pages so that they are accessible to all people, regardless of their abilities or disabilities.

18. Frontend Web Development:
- Development of the visible part of a website that interacts directly with users. It involves HTML, CSS and JavaScript.

19. Backend Web Development:
- Development of the non-visible part of a website that manages logic and data manipulation. It involves the use of languages such as PHP, Python or Node.js.

-END-

www.ingramcontent.com/pod-product-compliance
Lightning Source LLC
LaVergne TN
LVHW081530050326
832903LV00025B/1720